D1058845

A Person From Britain Whose Head Was the Shape of a Mitten

and other Limericks

by

N. M. Bodecker

illustrated by the author

A MARGARET K. MCELDERRY BOOK

Atheneum 1980 *New York*

OTHER BOOKS BY N. M. BODECKER

It's Raining Said John Twaining
The Mushroom Center Disaster
Let's Marry Said the Cherry
Hurry, Hurry, Mary Dear!

(MARGARET K. MCELDERRY BOOKS)

Library of Congress Cataloging in Publication Data
Bodecker, NM
A person from Britain and other limericks.
"A Margaret K. McElderry book."
SUMMARY: Absurd limericks by the well known Danish-American author and illustrator.
1. Limericks—Juvenile literature. [1. Limericks] I. Title.
PN6231.L5B53 811'.5'4 79-22779 ISBN 0-689-50152-8

Published simultaneously in Canada by McClelland & Stewart, Ltd.
Manufactured by American Book—Stratford Press, Inc.
Saddlebrook, New Jersey
First Edition

To Elsie and Cecil Lyon

A PERSON FROM BRITAIN

There was an old person from Britain
whose head was the shape of a mitten.
"You're handsome!" they said,
shaking hands with his head,
"you woolly old person from Britain."

PITCHER McDOWELL

A farm team pitcher, McDowell,
pitched an egg at a batter named Owl.
They cried: "Get a hit!"
but it hatched in the mitt
—and the umpire called it a "fowl!"

A MAN IN GUAM

A messy old man in Guam
got his waistcoat all covered with jam.
When they said: "What a sight!"
he replied: "You are right
—I forgot to put toast on my jam."

A GARDENER'S ROSES

A kindly old gardener's roses
grew some large, very cumbersome noses
which got sniffles (from dew)
so each morning he blew
with his hankie his rosebushes' noses.

A LADY OF VENICE

A little old lady of Venice
said she didn't care tenpins for tennis,
but when asked: "Will you play?"
got so carried away
she turned into a little old menace.

A COOK WHOSE DISHES

There was an old mess cook whose dishes
his customers fed to some fishes.
When the fish said: "Why us?"
they all said: "Bec'use
these are wonderful dishes for fishes."

A CRUSTY MECHANIC

There was an old crusty mechanic
whose manners were fierce and tyrannic:
dull headlights would glare
at his furious stare,
—and dead engines turn over in panic!

A BOA FROM GOA

A boa constrictor from Goa
frustrated an old man named Noah,
who cried: "I've been tricked!
It just *will* not constrict,
that obstructive constrictor from Goa!"

MURDOCH OF MUGG

Wicked old Murdoch of Mugg
made people who saw him say: "Ugh!
Here comes in his wig
on his ornery pig
that plug-ugly Murdoch of Mugg!"

A TALENTED DUCKLING

A modest but talented duckling
constructed a small clock, or clockling,
that went QUACK! when it struck,
like an old daddy duck,
which set all his duckling friends chuckling.

A WOMAN OF WARE

A poor but good woman of Ware,
who had no worldly goods she could spare,
when some birds came along
said: "Dear birds, for a song
I will make you a nest of my hair."

A GARD'NER WHOSE PLANTS . . .

There was an old gard'ner whose plants
were being consumed by some ants.
When he cried: "Oh, my garden!"
they said: "Beg your pardon,"
and quickly devoured his pants.

A MAN OF COLOGNE

There was an old man of Cologne,
his hair was the shape of a cone,
and his head was like ice,
but it didn't taste nice,
so they left that old ice man alone.

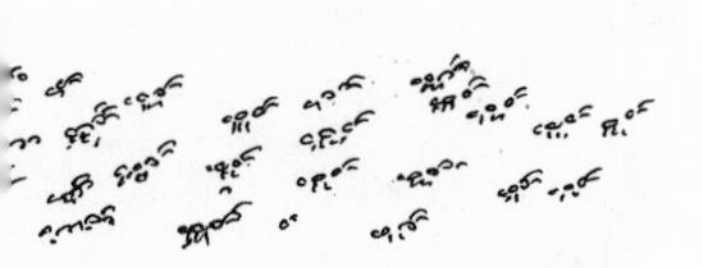

A MAID OF GREAT BADDOW

A sprightly young maid of Great Baddow
reached the end of her rope with her shadow.
"Don't crowd me," cried she,
"for I want to be free!"
and left it that night in Great Baddow.

A PERSON OF RAME

A rather vague person of Rame
just could not remember her name.
When someone from Scones
said: "My name is Jones,"
she said: "Oh? Perhaps mine is the same."

A DRIVER FROM DEERING

A school bus driver from Deering
disconcertingly kept disappearing:
he would head for Cape May,
but end up in Bombay
—because something was wrong with the steering

A MAN OF PENNANG

An honest old man of Pennang
once borrowed a friend's boomerang.
"I'll return it," he cried,
and he tried and he tried
—but it always came back to Pennang.

A MAN IN A SUIT

There was a young man in a suit
Whose fiancée thought him too cute,
so she messed up his tie
with a gleam in her eye
—and stuffed his hat into his boot.

A PERSON OF PINSK

There was a young person of Pinsk
who went with his mother to Minsk.
When she said: "We are there!"
he replied: "We are where?"
that depressing young person of Pinsk.

A HOUND OF COHASSET

An elderly hound of Cohasset,
introducing himself as a basset,
was told: "It's too bad
that your face looks so sad,"
but replied: "My sad face is my asset."

A LADY IN PLUMMER

A little old lady in Plummer
said: "I really wish it was summer."
When they said: "But it is,"
she replied: "It's a fizz!"
And never came back to Plummer.

A VIPER NAMED SAM

A lonely young viper named Sam
said to himself: "Here I am
without daddy or mummy,
out flat on my tummy,
and all people tell me is SCRAM!"

A MAID IN OLD LYME

A giddy young maid in Old Lyme
stuffed a new pillow with thyme
and said to her cat:
"Now, Tabbycat, that
should get us to bed on thyme."

KING JOHAN OF BAVONIA

Good King Johan of Bavonia
grew a most perfect begonia,
but it smelled of blue cheese,
which disgusted the bees,
which depressed that dear King of Bavonia.

GERONOMO HACKET

Good old Geronomo Hacket
had a bracket for hanging his jacket.
This was practical, but
he sometimes forgot
to take himself out of his jacket.

A PERSON IN ROME

There was a bald person in Rome
whose skull was as vast as a dome.
"You'll get chill-brains," they said,
insulating his head
with tar shingles, glass wool and foam.

A POOR MAN WHOSE PAJAMAS . . .

There was a poor man whose pajamas
were purloined, alas, by two llamas
who lounged on his bed
saying: "Pard'n us, Fred,
but please don't create any dramas."

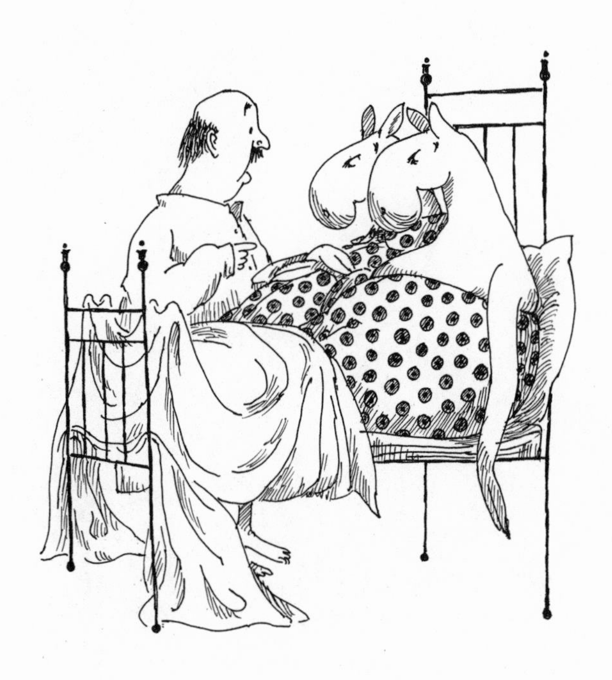

A FARMER OF CWM

A quiet old farmer of Cwm
discovered that he couldn't swm.
He fell into a wll
near the village of Dll
—and that's what is known about hm.

A MAID IN NEW YORK

A pretty young maid in New York
one morning turned into a stork.
When her dad said: "Too bad–"
she said to him: "Dad,
what *do* you expect in New York?"

A MAN OF THE DUNES

A delicious old man of the dunes
dined sweetly on beach plums and prunes,
and danced by the ocean
in lovely slow motion
while humming the yummiest tunes.

A MAN IN NORTHCHAPEL

A determined young man in Northchapel
kept the doctor away with an apple,
or rather with sacks
of Baldwins and Mac's
and every available apple!

A BAKER IN FRANCE

A poor, honest baker in France
asked some ladies to join in a dance.
When the ladies said: "NO!"
he danced with his dough,
not giving those spoilsports a glance.

A KIRGIZE IN A YURT

A kirgize who lived in a yurt
had nothing to wear but a shirt.
When they asked him to tea
he exclaimed: "Dearie me!"
and went there wearing his yurt.

TRAVELERS LUGGING VALISES

Some travelers lugging valises
said: "Sir, could you tell us where Greece is?"
When he said: "But I'm Swiss,"
they said: "Then tell us this:
how *do* you make holes in your cheeses?"

A TRAVELER FOR DAKOTA

A traveler bound for Dakota
said: "I frankly don't care one iota,
not a pin, not a jot,
if it's North, South or what.
I'll settle for *any* Dakota."

A BRIDE OF NORTH CONWAY

There was a young bride of North Conway,
whose veil was as long as a runway,
so they marked it with tags,
flares, blinkers and flags,
and a neat little sign saying, "ONE WAY."

A LASS ON BEN NEVIS

There was a young lass on Ben Nevis,
whose nose had got stuck in a crevice.
When it wouldn't come out
they said: "Without doubt
she'll remain all her days on Ben Nevis."

A MAN IN KARACHI

A wicked old man in Karachi
wore something quite horribly scratchy.
When he dropped what he wore
he was scratchy no more,
and the nicest old man in Karachi.

A GUARD AT FORT KNOX

A suspicious old guard at Fort Knox
kept all his hard cash in his socks,
but his feet got so sore
he decided to store
cash, socks and himself in a box.

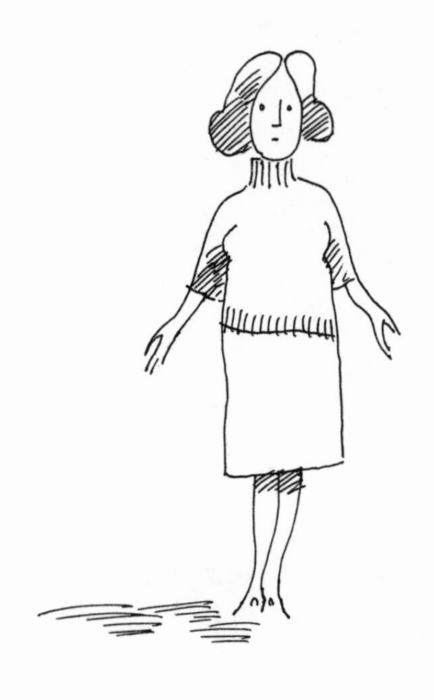

A PERSON OF KEENE

This middle-aged person of Keene
is neither too fat nor too lean,
not too good, not too bad,
neither happy nor sad,
but content to be somewhere between.

A LASS FROM MILWAUKEE

This far-roaming lass from Milwaukee
walked all the way to and from Gorki.
They admired her walk,
but said: "Boy, does she *talk*
—that unstoppable Milwaukee-talkie!"

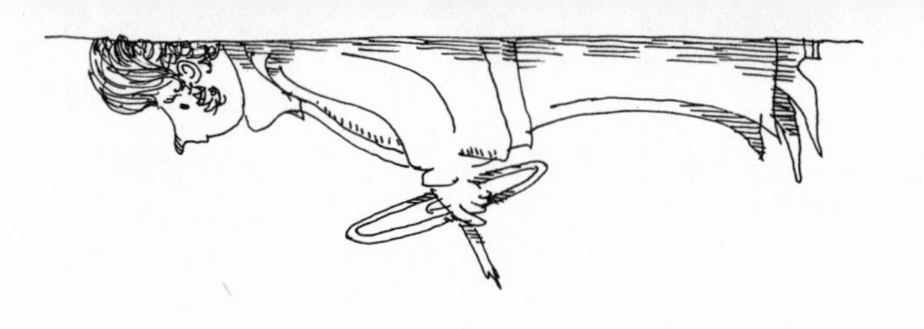

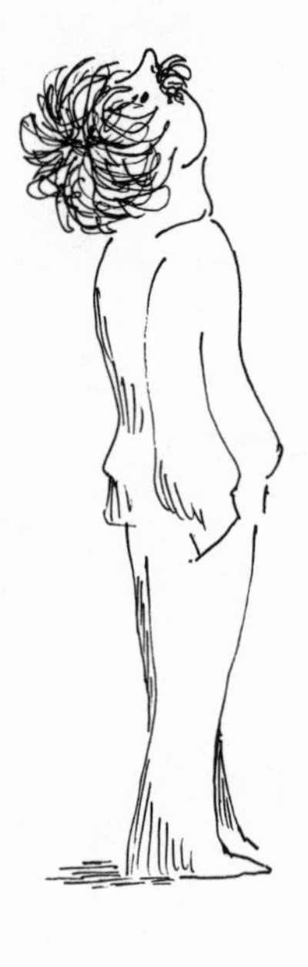

A PERSON OF EALING

A certain young person of Ealing
delighted in automobiling,
till someone named Hall
drove *him* up the wall,
—and parked him under the ceiling.

A LADY IN MADRID

A lady who lived in Madrid
made soup a way no one else did:
she swallowed some broth
with some herbs wrapped in cloth,
and covered her head with a lid.

A PERSON NAMED BRIGGS

There was a young person named Briggs,
whose hair grew like branches and twigs.
When she watered her toes
with a small garden hose,
it produced the most wonderful figs.

A PERSON IN SKYE

There was a young person in Skye,
who seemed rather excessively shy.
When they said to her: "Dear,
you have nothing to fear,"
she buried her head in a pie.

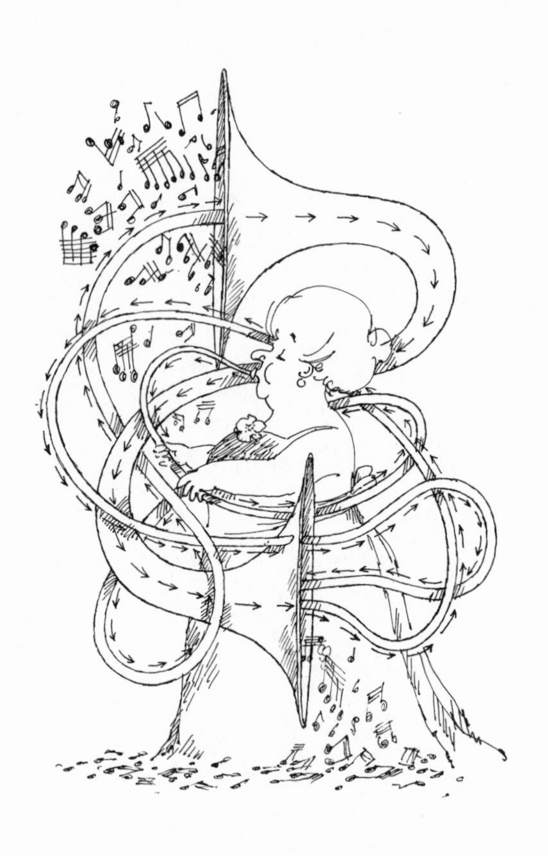

A PERSON IN ARUBA

A person of taste in Aruba
played a highly unusual tuba.
When they asked: "From Peru?"
she said: "No. Timbuktoo.
It's a regular Timbuktootuba."

A PERSON IN SPAIN

An indignant young person in Spain
looked out at a gray, grimy rain
and cried: "Will you clear!
Who told *you* to come here?
You horrible **Old English Rain.**"

A MAN IN A TREE

A furious man in a tree
said: "What's all this nature to me?
I have looked at the view.
Now what do I do?
I ought to have brung my TV."

AN EXPLORER NAMED BLISS

An intrepid explorer named Bliss
fell into a gorge or abyss,
but remarked as he fell:
"Oh I might just as well
get to the bottom of this . . ."

A PERSON OF DEEPING

A tearful young person of Deeping
one night said: "I must stop this weeping,
or else, I suppose,
learn to hang by my toes
so as not to be drowned while I'm sleeping."

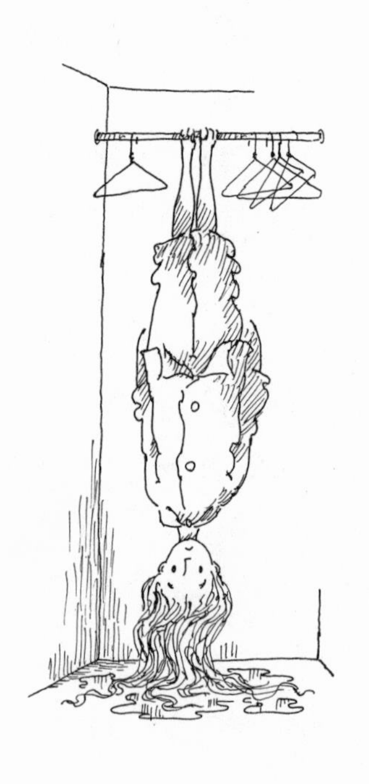

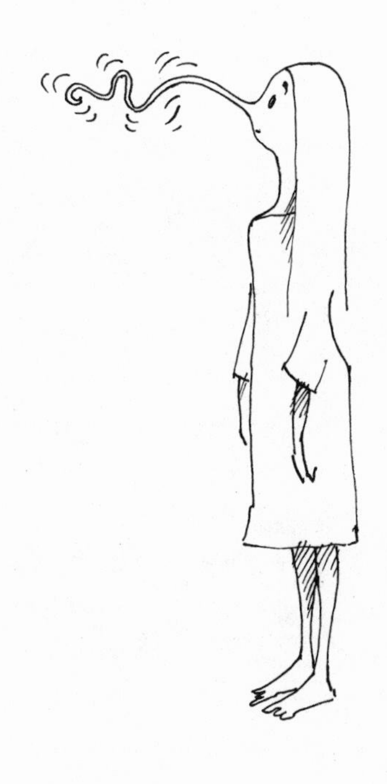

A PERSON IN STIRLING

A silly young person in Stirling
desired her hair to be curling.
Despite curlers and creams
it got straighter, it seems
—but her nose started twisting and twirling.

A PERSON OF HAXEY

A splendiferous person of Haxey,
whose mustaches were pointy and waxy,
tied flags left and right
(and lanterns at night)
to the points when he traveled by taxi.

A SHEIK FROM RIFF

A sheik from the mountains of Riff,
returned from a journey, said: "If
camels had wheels
like automobiles,
I would surely be feeling less stiff."

A PERSON IN CORNING

A tiresome person in Corning
just would not get up in the morning.
When they said: "Tell us why?"
she made some reply
—though they couldn't hear what for her yawning.

A PERSON OF FLORENCE

A horrid old person of Florence
regarded most things with abhorrence:
he thought hummingbirds dumb;
he could not abide gum;
and cared nothing for Tom, Dick or Florence.

A PERSON OF NIGG

A little old person of Nigg
displayed a most far-reaching wig.
When they said: "You're too small,"
he replied: "Not at all,
it's the wig, I suspect, that's too big."

Index